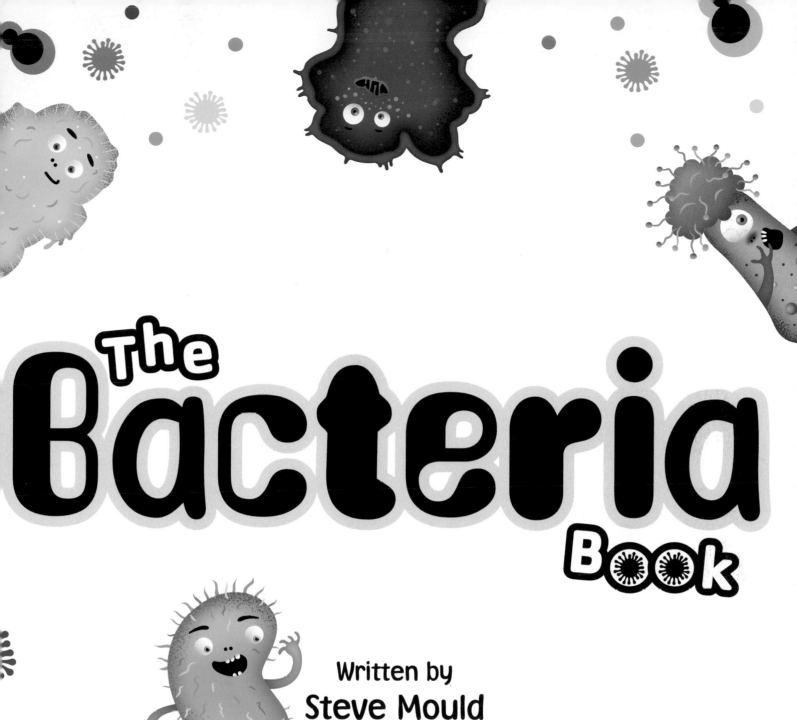

The Bacteria Book

Written by
Steve Mould

Contents

DK | Penguin Random House

Written by Steve Mould
Consultant Edward Marks, PhD

Editor Allison Singer
Senior designer Joanne Clark
Design assistant Ala Uddin

Additional editorial Olivia Stanford,
Sam Priddy, Amina Youssef
Illustration Mark Clifton, Molly Lattin,
Bettina Myklebust Stovne
Jacket designer Joanne Clark
Managing editor Laura Gilbert
Managing art editor Diane Peyton Jones
Pre-production producer Rob Dunn
Senior producer Isabell Schart
Art director Martin Wilson
Creative director Helen Senior
Publishing director Sarah Larter

There are some **tricky words** in this book! Do your best to sound them out, then turn to the **glossary** to see if you got them right.

First American Edition, 2018
Published in the United States by DK Publishing
345 Hudson Street, New York, New York 10014

Copyright © 2018 Dorling Kindersley Limited
DK, a Division of Penguin Random House LLC
18 19 20 21 22 10 9 8 7 6 5 4 3 2
002–307940–May/2018

DK books are available at special discounts when purchased in bulk for sales promotions, premiums, fund-raising, or educational use. For details, contact: DK Publishing Special Markets, 345 Hudson Street, New York, New York 10014
SpecialSales@dk.com

A catalog record for this book is available from the Library of Congress.
ISBN: 978-1-4654-7028-7

Printed and bound in China

A WORLD OF IDEAS:
SEE ALL THERE IS TO KNOW

www.dk.com

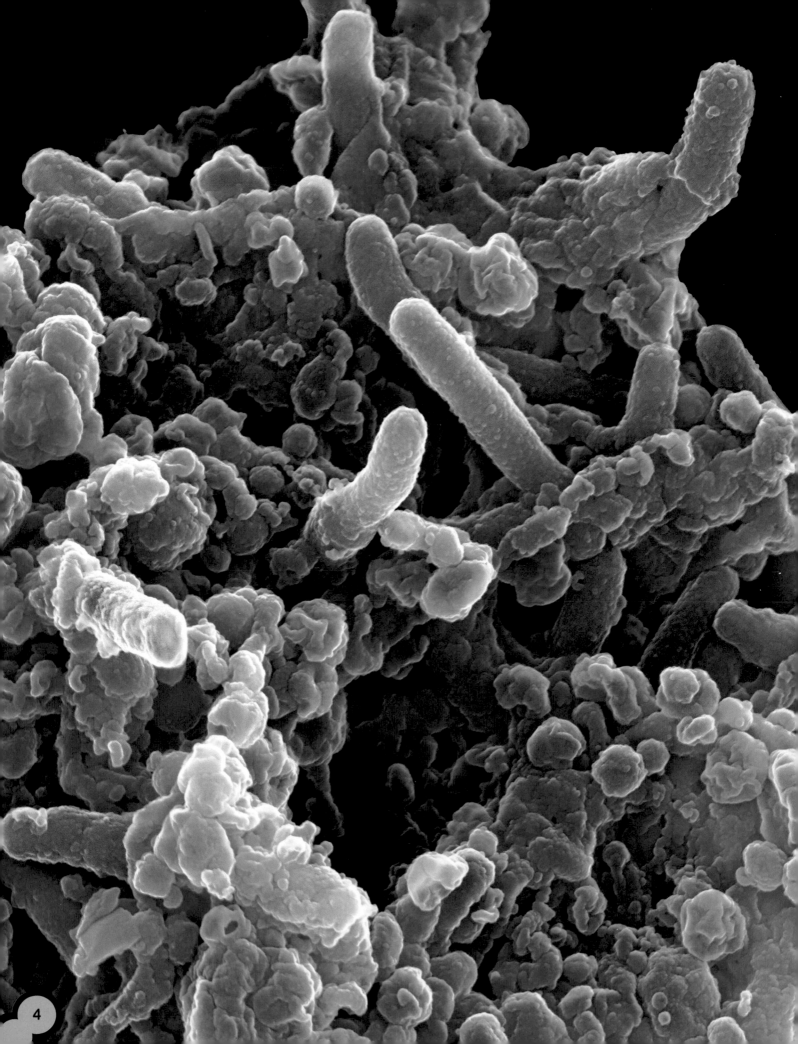

Introduction

Looking into a microscope is like peering into an **alien world**, one full of peculiar, pulsating creatures that act and move in strange ways. These **mysterious microbes** are absolutely everywhere—**around you, on you, and inside you**. We live in harmony with some of them, and we're at war with the rest.

Some of the creatures you'll find in this book are **gross** and terrifying, while others are simply **amazing**. Get ready to discover the bacteria that makes you fart, the mite that lives in your eyelashes, and the fungus that turns ants into zombies.

The world of the very small is **endlessly fascinating**, and I've packed these pages full of my favorite bits. Enjoy!

Steve Mould

What is a microbe?

A microorganism, or "microbe," is any **living creature** that is so small you can't see it with your eyes. The most common microbe is **bacteria**, which first appeared on Earth more than **3.6 billion years ago**.

There could be as many as **one trillion** species of microbe **on Earth.**

Smaller than rice

Just how small are these creatures? Zoom in three thousand times on a single grain of rice and you might start to see lots of little bacteria. Viruses, another type of microbe, are smaller still!

One grain of rice is about 0.25 in (6 mm) long.

GRAINS OF RICE ARE **THOUSANDS** OF TIMES LONGER THAN BACTERIA.

There are many bacteria on a grain of rice and in the air around it.

ACTUAL SIZE

The biggest bacteria are still tiny, at about 0.03 in (0.75 mm), the size of this blue dot.

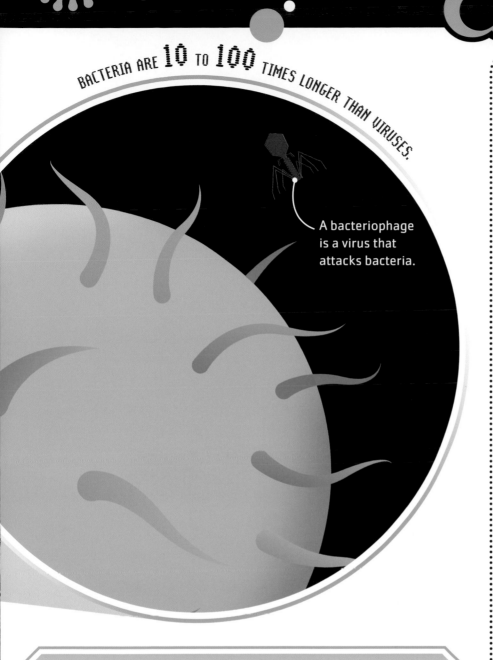

A bacteriophage is a virus that attacks bacteria.

ARE MICROBES REALLY ALIVE?

Although they are tiny, yes! Scientists don't agree on what makes something alive, but all living things seem to share certain features, such as the ability to move and to grow. Viruses only have some of these features, however, so some people think they *aren't* alive.

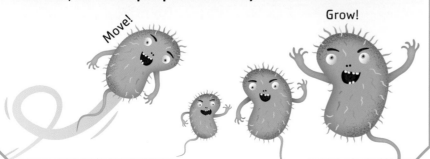

Move!

Grow!

If you were a microbe...

If you were shrunk down to the size of bacteria, a grain of rice would seem bigger than a mountain. That's how small microbes are. Can you imagine it?

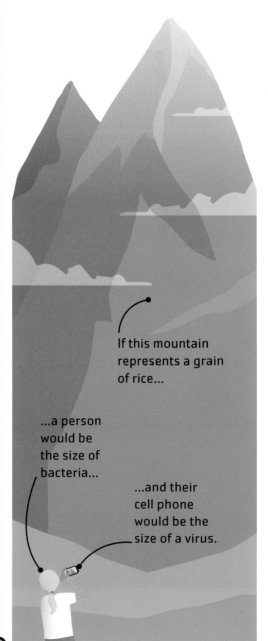

If this mountain represents a grain of rice...

...a person would be the size of bacteria...

...and their cell phone would be the size of a virus.

Meet the microbes

Say "hello" to the **smallest critters on Earth**! Here are six of the most common types of microbe. These creatures **are everywhere you look**— even though you usually can't see them.

Bacteria

Bacteria are made of just one cell each, and they are the simplest cells on the planet. There are more bacteria on Earth than any other form of life.

Bacteria come in different shapes. These ones are rod-shaped.

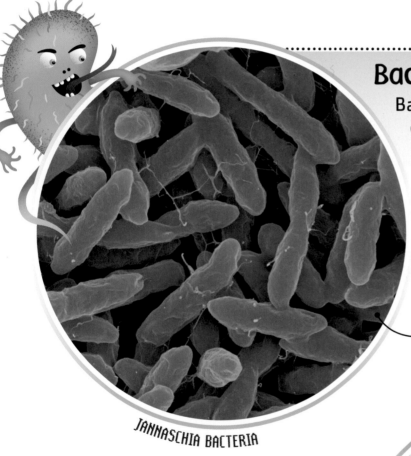

JANNASCHIA BACTERIA

BACTERIOPHAGE VIRUS

Viruses

Viruses are the smallest microbes. They are so small, they live inside the cells of other creatures. Many scientists say viruses may not even be alive since they don't eat or grow.

This virus is attaching itself to a bacteria cell.

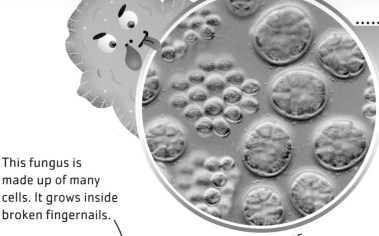

Algae

Many algae are made of one cell each, but they are usually bigger than bacteria. Like plants, algae use a green chemical called chlorophyll to turn sunlight into useful energy.

GREEN ALGAE

This fungus is made up of many cells. It grows inside broken fingernails.

This protozoa lives inside fish. When it moves, it looks like it's walking.

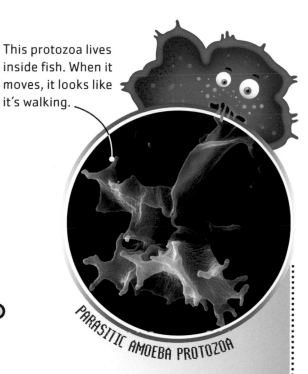

PARASITIC AMOEBA PROTOZOA

Fungi

Fungi, such as mold, break down dead plants and animals to use as food. A fungus can be made of one cell or of lots of cells.

SYNCEPHALASTRUM RACEMOSUM FUNGUS

Protozoa

Protozoa are made of only one cell. These creatures behave a bit like animals—they move around and eat other living things.

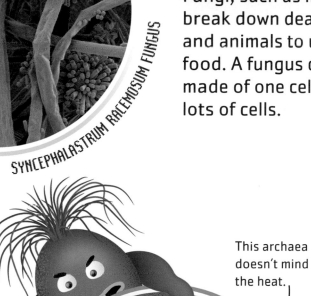

This archaea doesn't mind the heat.

Archaea

Archaea look a lot like bacteria, but they behave in different ways. They can survive in extreme environments, such as very hot places or strong acids.

HYPERTHERMOPHILE ARCHAEA

Seeing is **believing**

Microbes are creatures we can't see with just our eyes, so **how do we know** they exist? One way is by looking through a microscope—but this isn't the **only** way.

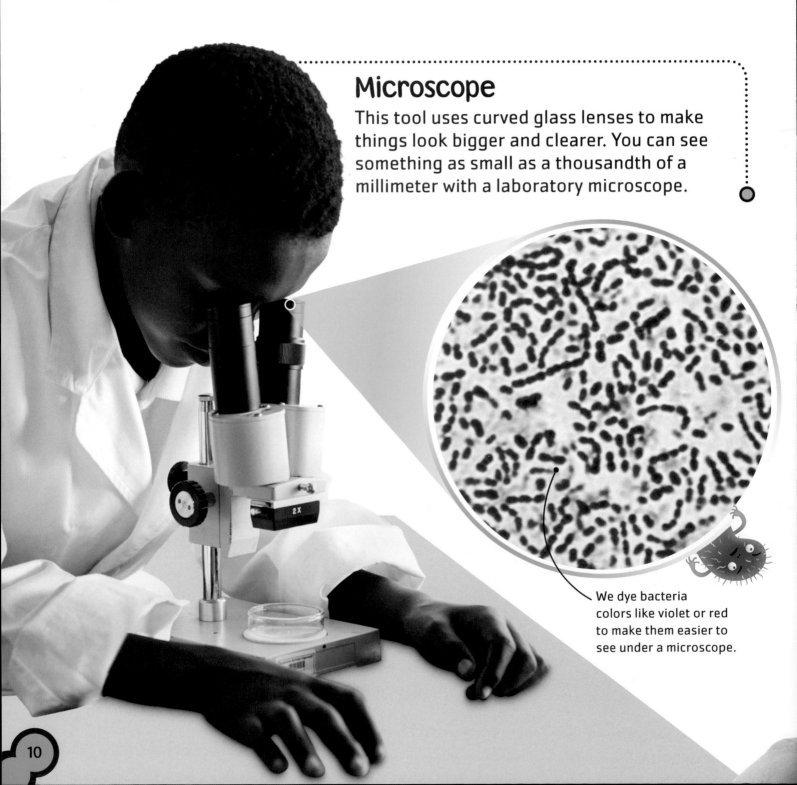

Microscope

This tool uses curved glass lenses to make things look bigger and clearer. You can see something as small as a thousandth of a millimeter with a laboratory microscope.

We dye bacteria colors like violet or red to make them easier to see under a microscope.

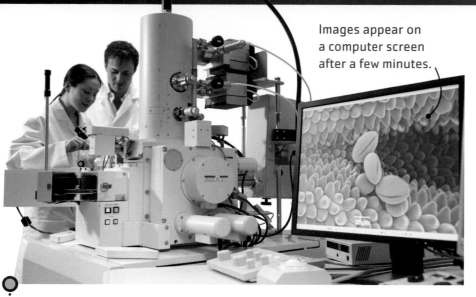

Images appear on a computer screen after a few minutes.

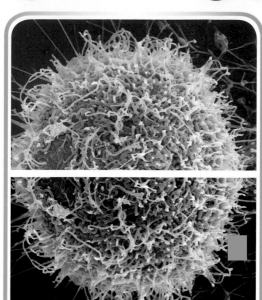

Electron microscope

Some microbes, such as viruses, are too small to be seen with a regular microscope. Scientists use a special tool called an electron microscope to fire tiny particles called electrons at the virus. The electrons help make a computer picture.

Colored pictures
Pictures made using an electron microscope are black-and-white. People add color to the images later to make them clearer.

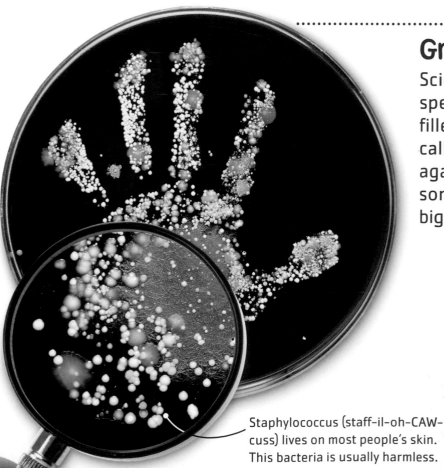

Growing blobs

Scientists make bacteria grow on special plates called petri dishes filled with a nutrient-rich goop called agar. The nutrients in the agar help the bacteria grow. After some time, the bacteria blobs are big enough for us to see.

Microbes that can **make people sick** are called **germs.**

Staphylococcus (staff-il-oh-CAW-cuss) lives on most people's skin. This bacteria is usually harmless.

Animal cells

Look at your skin under a microscope and you'll see it's made of cells. We don't think of them as being alive because they can't grow and reproduce on their own. The cells in your body work together to keep the whole organism alive.

When a skin cell is separated from your body, it dies. It can no longer grow or reproduce.

Skin cells work together to form a protective barrier for your body.

The human body is made of about **30 trillion cells.**

All about cells

When you think of living creatures, or organisms, you probably think of animals and plants, not **microscopic blobs**. But all living creatures have something in common, from the **biggest mammal** to the **smallest bacteria**: They are all made of cells.

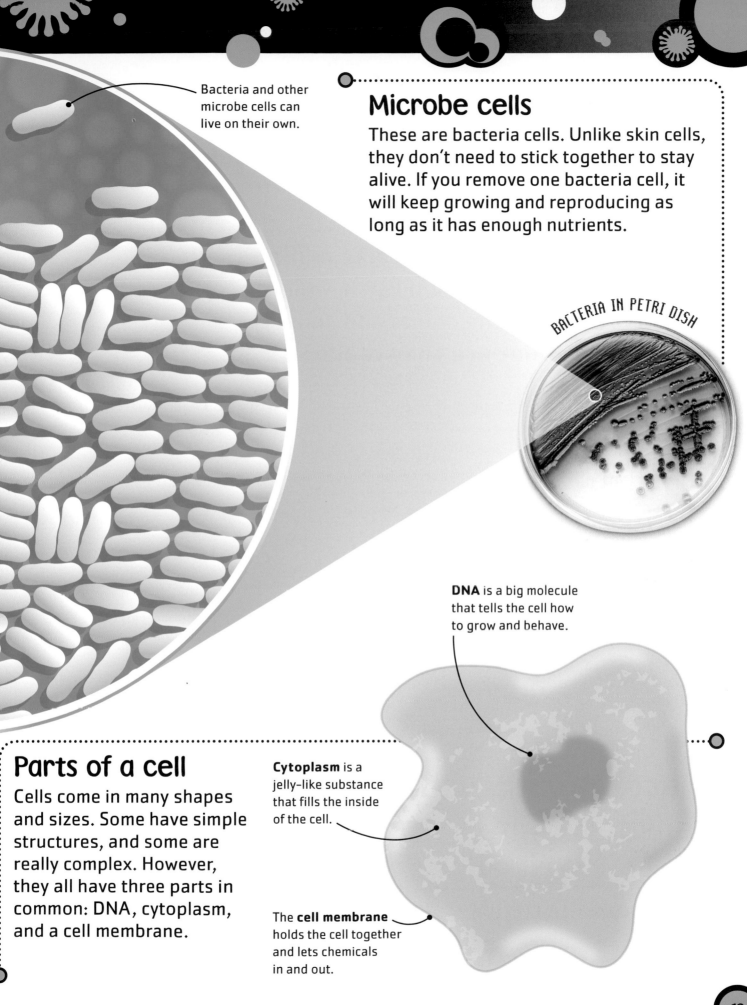

Bacteria and other microbe cells can live on their own.

Microbe cells

These are bacteria cells. Unlike skin cells, they don't need to stick together to stay alive. If you remove one bacteria cell, it will keep growing and reproducing as long as it has enough nutrients.

BACTERIA IN PETRI DISH

DNA is a big molecule that tells the cell how to grow and behave.

Parts of a cell

Cells come in many shapes and sizes. Some have simple structures, and some are really complex. However, they all have three parts in common: DNA, cytoplasm, and a cell membrane.

Cytoplasm is a jelly-like substance that fills the inside of the cell.

The **cell membrane** holds the cell together and lets chemicals in and out.

What are bacteria?

There are **millions of bacteria** in a teaspoon of pond water or a pinch of soil. About **five million trillion trillion** bacteria are alive on Earth, which together weigh more than all the plants and animals combined. But **what are they really**?

Bacteria cell

Every bacteria is made of one cell. The inside of a bacteria cell is much simpler than the cells of other living things.

The extra layer of protection around the cell is called the **cell wall**.

Some bacteria have little hairs called **pili**. They use their pili to attach to surfaces.

Bacteria with tails can swim **100 times** their own length in **one second**.

This is the **cell membrane**. It lets in nutrients that help the cell grow, and lets out waste the cell doesn't need.

Shaping up

Bacteria come in many shapes and sizes. Here are the most common.

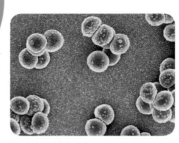

Cocci
Cocci bacteria are round or oval, like balls.

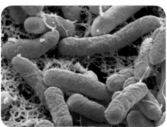

Bacilli
Bacilli bacteria are shaped like little pills or rods.

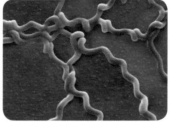

Spirilla
Spirella bacteria are long and twisty, like a corkscrew.

Some bacteria have a spinning tail called a **flagellum** that propels them forward.

This long, tangled string is called **DNA**. It stores information about what the cell is and how it works.

Cytoplasm is the thick gel that fills the cell.

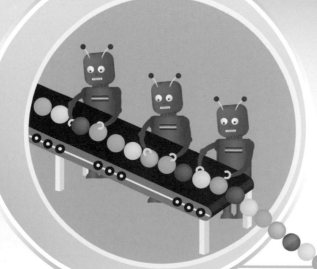

INSIDE A RIBOSOME

BUILDING BACTERIA

Floating in the cytoplasm of a bacteria cell are little molecules called ribosomes. Ribosomes are like tiny factories. They "read" bits of copied DNA like an instruction manual, then use the instructions to build parts for the cell that they're in.

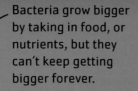

Bacteria grow bigger by taking in food, or nutrients, but they can't keep getting bigger forever.

The cell then splits in the middle to make two new cells, with one copy of the DNA in each.

The two new cells are identical. With enough nutrients, they will both grow and split, making four cells.

When a bacteria cell gets to a certain size, it makes a copy of its DNA. The two copies move to separate ends of the cell.

Every time the cells split, the total number of cells doubles. This time four cells become eight.

The power of doubling

An E. coli bacteria cell takes 20 minutes to split into two. That may sound slow, but with enough food, each of the new cells will also double after 20 minutes—then again, and again, until one cell becomes billions.

Eight cells become 16...

Growing and **dividing**

Bacteria and other organisms made of just one cell **reproduce**, or create new organisms, by **dividing into two copies** of themselves. Through this process, one little bacteria cell can **quickly turn into many**!

PERFECT CONDITIONS

Bacteria grow faster when the conditions are just right. They like lots of moisture, warmth, and nutrients. Scientists can create these conditions in a petri dish to grow bacteria they want to study.

...16 cells become 32...

...32 cells become 64...

...and 64 cells become 128.

After 12 hours, **one bacteria cell** can grow and divide **into 70 billion!**

Where in the world?

Where can you find bacteria? The short answer is... **everywhere**! Wherever you look, you'll find them doing **amazing things**. Here are just a few places you can go hunting for bacteria.

A person carries **about 4.4 lb (2 kg) of bacteria** in and on their body.

Rocks

Some bacteria can survive inside rocks. There isn't much there to eat, so they grow slowly and reproduce only every 100 years or so.

Air and sky

There are bacteria floating in the air around you, as well as in the atmosphere up above your head. Some bacteria even live inside clouds!

Ocean

Bacteria are found at all depths of the ocean. At the surface, they take in energy from the sun. On the ocean floor, they get energy from chemicals.

Soil

Soil is jam-packed with bacteria. The bacteria that live in soil can turn nitrogen in the air into useful nutrients for plants. This is part of a process called the nitrogen cycle.

Nitrogen cycle

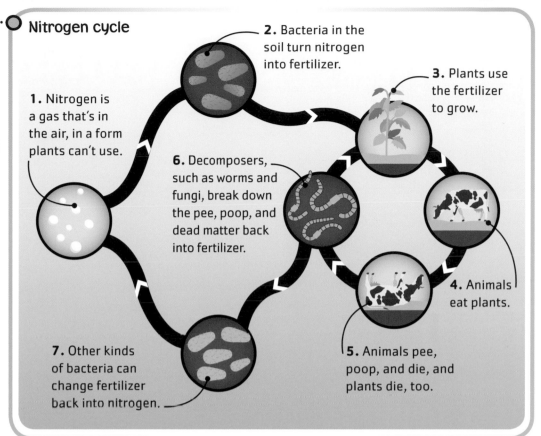

1. Nitrogen is a gas that's in the air, in a form plants can't use.

2. Bacteria in the soil turn nitrogen into fertilizer.

3. Plants use the fertilizer to grow.

4. Animals eat plants.

5. Animals pee, poop, and die, and plants die, too.

6. Decomposers, such as worms and fungi, break down the pee, poop, and dead matter back into fertilizer.

7. Other kinds of bacteria can change fertilizer back into nitrogen.

At home

Your home is full of bacteria, but don't worry—most of them are completely harmless. You might find some dangerous ones on surfaces that aren't properly cleaned.

In you!

Bacteria play a big role in your body and on your skin. In fact, there are more bacteria cells in your body than human cells!

19

Look inside

Bobtail squid have special bacteria living in them. Chemicals inside the bacteria make them light up. This is called bioluminescence.

Can a squid glow?

The **bobtail squid** is an amazing animal. It lives in the shallow waters of the Pacific and Indian oceans. At first glance, it **appears to be glowing**! Can you guess what is really making it shine?

Bacteria help the squid hide from animals below by matching the brightness of the waters above.

Bobtail squid grow to about **1.2 in** (30 mm) long. That's **seven times smaller** than the average squid.

LIGHT IT UP

Bobtail squid aren't the only living creatures that glow in the dark. Check out these other super shiners.

Mushrooms
When fungi like mushrooms make light, we call it fox fire. They use their green glow to ward off hungry predators.

Anglerfish
Female anglerfish have a body part full of glowing bacteria on their heads. It helps them lure in prey and find mates.

Plankton
These waves crashing on to a beach in the Maldives, South Asia, are full of tiny bioluminescent plankton. The light confuses their predators.

In your body

Humans are born with a **bit of bacteria**, but our bodies are quickly inhabited by hundreds of species. Although we often think of bacteria as **evil critters that make us sick**, most are harmless—and some are even helpful.

What's that smell?

Most of the bacteria in your body can be found in your gut, where they help you to digest, or break down, your food. But they also have an embarrassing side effect—one you may notice if you eat too many beans...

1 **Mouth**
The first step is chewing! Food must be broken down into smaller parts before it can be used by your body.

Throat

Muscles in your throat push the food into your stomach.

Stomach acid

2 **Stomach**
Food is broken down further by acid in your stomach. The resulting goop is then passed to your small intestine.

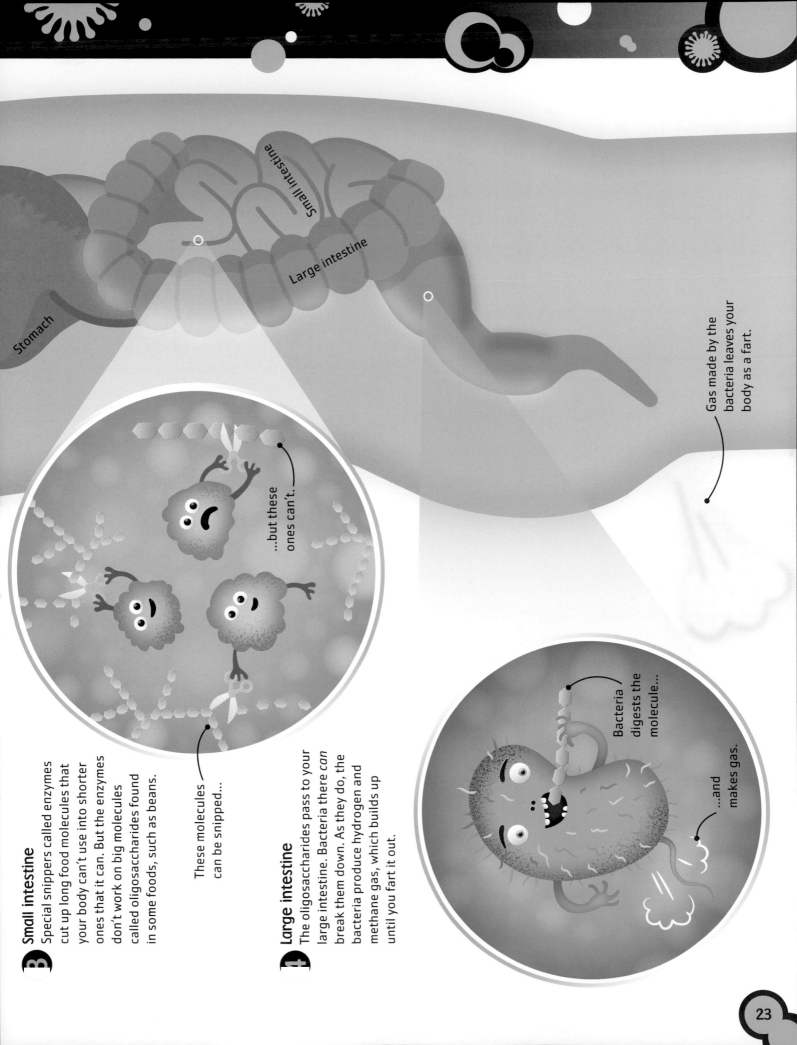

Stomach

Small intestine

Large intestine

Gas made by the bacteria leaves your body as a fart.

...but these ones can't.

These molecules can be snipped...

B Small intestine

Special snippers called enzymes cut up long food molecules that your body can't use into shorter ones that it can. But the enzymes don't work on big molecules called oligosaccharides found in some foods, such as beans.

4 Large intestine

The oligosaccharides pass to your large intestine. Bacteria there *can* break them down. As they do, the bacteria produce hydrogen and methane gas, which builds up until you fart it out.

Bacteria digests the molecule...

...and makes gas.

The bad guys

Most bacteria are harmless. Some are even helpful. But some can cause us to **feel unwell**. These **harmful bacteria** have clever ways of getting from one human host to the next.

About **half the weight** of your poop is bacteria.

Cholera

Cholera is a terrible illness that spreads easily in places where the drinking water is not clean. In 1855, scientist John Snow discovered that a cholera outbreak in London, England, was caused by something in the water.

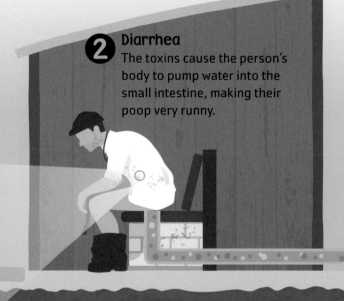

2 Diarrhea
The toxins cause the person's body to pump water into the small intestine, making their poop very runny.

3 Cesspool
In the 1800s in London, the toilets emptied into underground cesspools. Watery diarrhea helped the cholera bacteria flow easily through any cracks in the cesspool wall.

1 Bacteria multiply
Cholera bacteria multiply inside the warm, moist digestive system of its victim. They attach themselves to the lining of the small intestine and release dangerous chemicals called toxins.

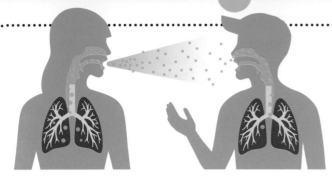

Whooping cough

Whooping cough bacteria causes a sticky substance called mucus to build up in the lungs. The victim must cough to clear it. This sprays bacteria into the air, and other people breathe it in.

Acne

Acne bacteria live harmlessly inside little holes in your skin called follicles. When a follicle gets blocked, the bacteria feed on oils that build up, and multiply. Your body fights back with red swelling called inflammation—a pimple!

Once John Snow realized what was making people ill, the water pump was shut off.

5 **Contaminated water**
When people drank well water contaminated with cholera bacteria, they became infected.

6 **Symptoms pass on**
This new victim now has diarrhea, too! She will add more cholera bacteria to the cesspool.

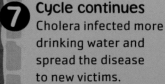

4 **Infected water supply**
Cholera bacteria seeped through cracks into an underground well. Before people had tap water, they would pump water from wells for drinking.

7 **Cycle continues**
Cholera infected more drinking water and spread the disease to new victims.

25

Your body's defenses

Your body has all sorts of **ways to defend itself** against harmful microbes, or germs. Together, these defenses make up your **immune system**. Your immune system's first line of defense is your skin.

Dangerous bacteria and germs can't get through your skin.

When you get a cut, your immune system sends more bacteria-fighting blood to the area, causing your skin to become red and swollen.

Cut

Your skin is your biggest organ. It's a tough layer of armor around your body. When it's cut, the tissue underneath is exposed to germs, which can cause infection.

The blood in your body flows through a system of tubes called arteries.

Inside your blood are different types of white blood cells, all with different ways of fighting germs.

ALLERGIES

When your immune system attacks something that isn't harmful, such as pollen, it's called an allergy. Having an allergy to pollen is called hay fever.

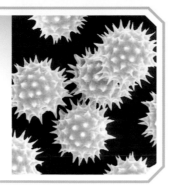

Macrophage

This incredible sight is a type of white blood cell called a macrophage. It engulfs germs and tears them apart using chemicals called enzymes.

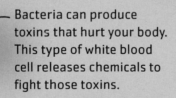

Bacteria can produce toxins that hurt your body. This type of white blood cell releases chemicals to fight those toxins.

This kind of white blood cell releases chemicals called antibodies that kill or stun invading germs. Then the macrophages can easily gobble them up.

OTHER DEFENSES

Your immune system has a few other tricks that help to stop an infection in its tracks.

Fever

When you have a fever, your body temperature is higher than normal. Fevers fight germs and help white blood cells work better.

Sneezing

Microbes in your nose can make you sneeze. Sneezing helps to expel the germs, keeping you healthy.

Tears

Germs can irritate your eyes. The tears they cause try to flush them out.

The story of **antibiotics**

There are ways to avoid getting **infected by bacteria**, such as **washing your hands** and **not touching your eyes and mouth**. If you already have an infection, however, your doctor might give you medicine. Medicines that fight bacteria are called **antibiotics**.

Amazing discovery

There used to be no treatment for deadly bacterial infections such as pneumonia. Then, bacteriologist Alexander Fleming accidentally discovered something amazing.

In 1928, before leaving for a trip, Alexander Fleming set up bacteria samples to grow in petri dishes while he was away. When he returned, one sample looked very strange...

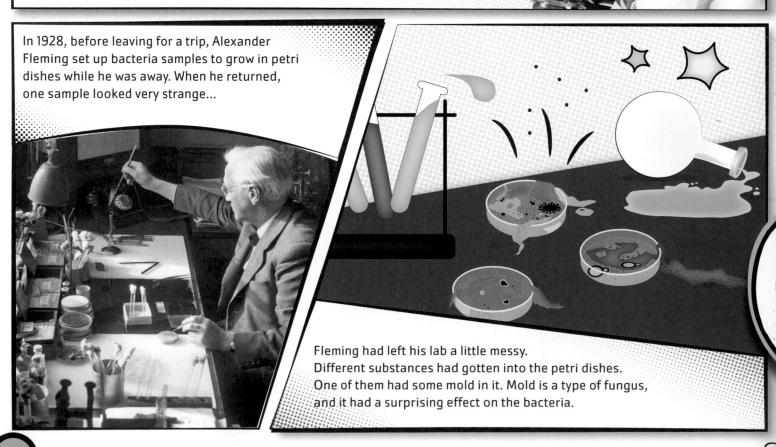

Fleming had left his lab a little messy. Different substances had gotten into the petri dishes. One of them had some mold in it. Mold is a type of fungus, and it had a surprising effect on the bacteria.

Fleming figured out what had happened. The hungry mold, called penicillium, had killed nearby bacteria competing for nutrients by releasing a molecule we now call **penicillin**. The penicillin had made the bacteria cells pop.

Pow! The penicillium fungus knocks out the bacteria cell. Fungus is the winner!

I win!

FLEMING'S PETRI DISH

Healthy bacteria

Popped bacteria

Penicillium mold

Over time, scientists figured out how to separate the penicillin from its mold. Penicillin is now used to treat bacteria infections all over the world.

Not so fast!

But then...
BACTERIA FIGHT BACK!

Bacteria don't give up easily. They can get used to an antibiotic, causing it to stop working. This is why scientists are always on the hunt for new antibiotics.

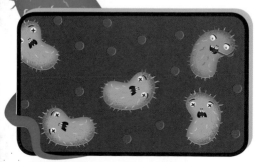

Antibiotic mostly works
An antibiotic can kill bacteria, but some cells that are slightly different, or mutated, survive.

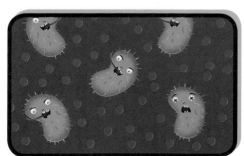

Antibiotic stops working
The mutated bacteria grow and multiply. The old antibiotic doesn't work too well on these bacteria.

New antibiotic works
New antibiotics are found that kill the mutated bacteria. But new mutations continue to form...

Bacteria with
superpowers

Bacteria have been around for nearly **four billion years**, and in that time they have developed some amazing abilities. Here are just a few of their **surprising superpowers**.

They're magnetic!

Magnetotactic (mag-neh-toh-TAK-tic) bacteria have a long string of magnetic crystals inside them that acts like a compass needle. The crystals help the bacteria to be able to point north.

They're electric!

Some bacteria, such as Shewanella (she-wah-NEHL-ah), grow little hairs that act like wires. The hairs pull electricity in and push it out. They even poop an electric charge!

They're super sticky!

The stickiest bacteria, Caulobacter crescentus (CALL-oh-bak-tur kreh-SEN-tuhs), is three times stronger than superglue. The "glue" that it produces is made of sugar.

Bacteria on a human tooth

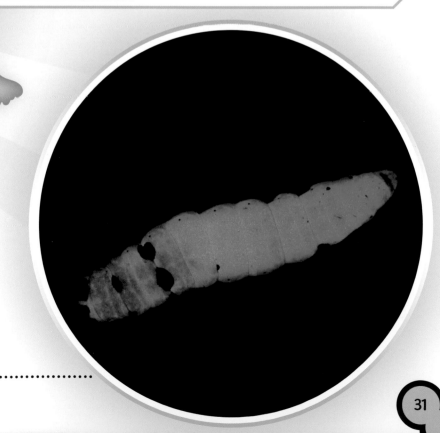

ON YOUR TEETH

Stickiness is common in bacteria. For example, some bacteria stick to your teeth and cause tooth decay. Did you know there are more bacteria in your mouth than there are people in the world?

They're dissolving!

Photorhabdus (fo-toh-RAB-duhs) bacteria can dissolve a caterpillar from the inside. This makes it edible for other creatures, such as the nematode worm that carries the bacteria around in its gut. Oh, and it glows!

Bacteria put to work

Humans have been using bacteria for **thousands of years** without knowing it—inside our bodies. Now, thanks to technology, we're finding lots of **creative new ways** to use bacteria.

Making medicine

Your pancreas makes a chemical called insulin that helps balance the amount of sugar in your blood. People with a disease called diabetes can't make enough insulin on their own, so they have to inject it. That's where bacteria comes in.

Before the bacteria method, people used insulin from a **pig's pancreas.**

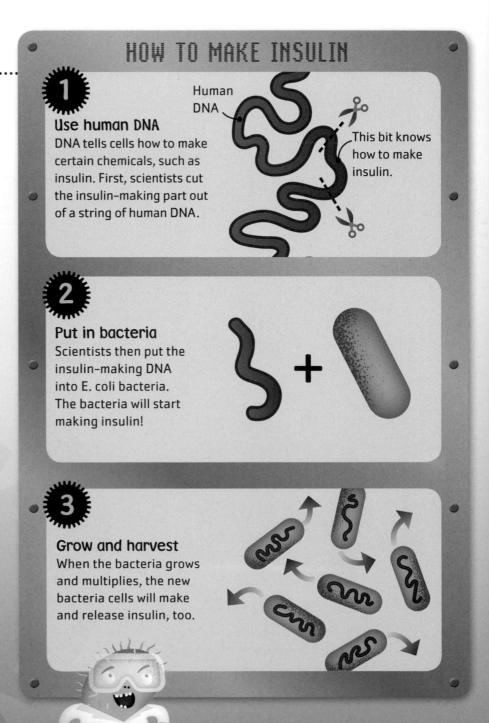

HOW TO MAKE INSULIN

1 Use human DNA
DNA tells cells how to make certain chemicals, such as insulin. First, scientists cut the insulin-making part out of a string of human DNA.

Human DNA

This bit knows how to make insulin.

2 Put in bacteria
Scientists then put the insulin-making DNA into E. coli bacteria. The bacteria will start making insulin!

3 Grow and harvest
When the bacteria grows and multiplies, the new bacteria cells will make and release insulin, too.

Helping hand

People use bacteria to make all sorts of products that make our world better, from growing hardy crops to helping us clean up our mistakes.

Insects are eating away at these crops.

These insect-resistant crops are healthier.

Cleaning clothes

Bacteria make molecules called enzymes that break down other molecules. We put these enzymes in laundry detergent to help break down stains in our clothes.

Protecting crops

Some plants can resist the insects that try to eat them. We can take instructions from these plants' DNA and copy it into bacteria, then put that bacteria into other plants to make them resistant, too.

Making materials

Scientists are experimenting with ways bacteria can be used to make building materials. For example, some bacteria can stick sand together to make bricks.

Oil spills are harmful for sea life, but bacteria help clean them up.

Eating oil

Bacteria in the ocean help clean up oil spilled by ships. People speed up this process by using chemicals to break the oil into tiny droplets the bacteria can eat more easily.

Living in bacteria

Unlike bacteria, viruses can't make copies of themselves, or reproduce, without help. They have to force the cells of another organism to do the copying for them. A bacteriophage is a type of virus that infects bacteria.

Instructions for building a copy of the virus are stored in its **DNA**.

These **tail fibers** help the virus attach to the bacteria cell.

The shell of a virus is called a **capsid**.

What is a
virus?

If you've ever had a cold, then you've been **infected by a virus**. Viruses are the simplest form of life and are much **smaller than bacteria**. They are responsible for lots of different diseases.

Bacteria cell wall

Bacteria cell membrane

Shapes

Viruses come in a variety of different shapes and sizes. Here are just a few examples.

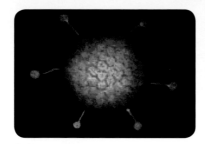

Adenovirus
Adenovirus affects breathing. Its shell is shaped like 20 triangles arranged into a ball.

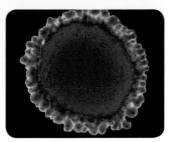

Influenza
Influenza, the flu virus, is wrapped in a layer of the infected person's skin.

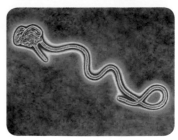

Ebola
Ebola is shaped like a curly tube. It is an incredibly deadly virus.

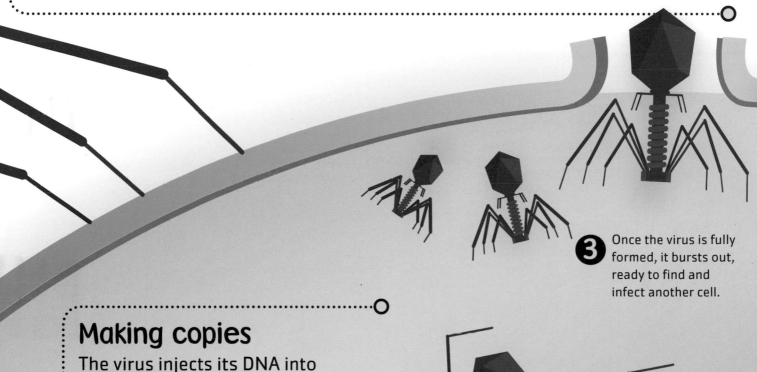

3 Once the virus is fully formed, it bursts out, ready to find and infect another cell.

Making copies

The virus injects its DNA into the bacteria cell. DNA is a really long molecule. It is a bit like an instruction manual because it holds all of the instructions for building copies of the virus.

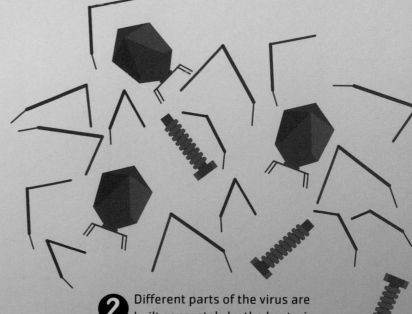

1 Special molecules inside the bacteria cell blindly follow the instructions held in the virus's DNA.

2 Different parts of the virus are built separately by the bacteria cell. Then they snap together.

Catching a cold

The common cold is a viral infection that gives you a runny nose, sore throat, and headache. The average child catches **seven colds a year**, which is more than any other infection.

Passing it on

To infect a new person, a cold virus must somehow get into the nose, eyes, or mouth of its next victim. As you'll see below, that's not hard to do!

➤➤ Colds are caused by more than 200 different viruses. The most common cold virus is the **rhinovirus**.

➤➤ There is no known cure for the common cold!

Cell infected with rhinovirus

1 **Wiping snot**
If someone with a cold wipes a runny nose, the cold virus is transferred to their hand.

2 **Touching hands**
Touching someone else's hand will transfer the virus to their hand.

3 **Eating food**
Touching your food transfers the virus from your skin to your snack.

The virus is in a sticky mucus called snot.

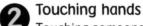

The virus is now on the apple!

BREAK THE CYCLE!

There are a few simple steps you can take to stop a common cold from spreading.

Eat and sleep well
Eating healthy foods, such as fruits and vegetables, and getting enough sleep will keep your body in top shape to fight viral infections.

Cover your mouth
Sneeze and cough into a tissue or the inside of your elbow, not your hand.

Wash your hands
Before touching your eyes, nose, or mouth, wash your hands with soap and water.

Stay home
If you have a cold, stay at home until you're better so you don't pass it on to others.

4 Getting sick
Once in your mouth, the virus can multiply, infect your cells, and make you sick.

5 Wiping snot
With snot on your hands, you will transfer the virus onto anything you touch.

6 The cycle continues
The virus can then pass onto its next victim.

Sneezing transfers the virus back to your hands.

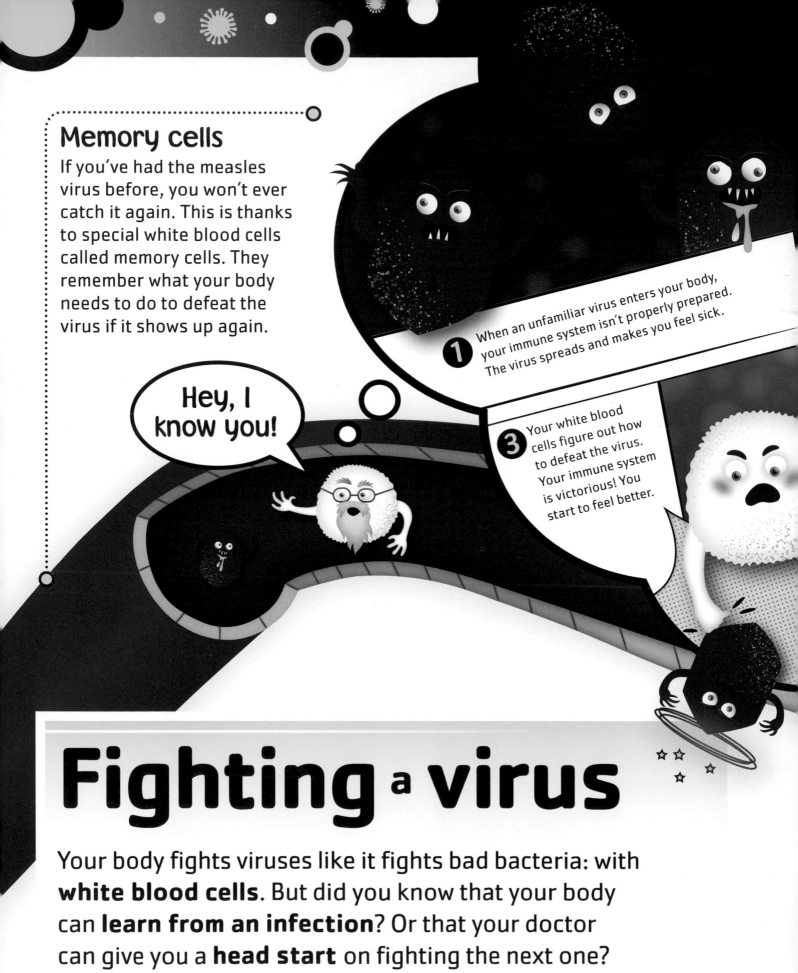

Memory cells

If you've had the measles virus before, you won't ever catch it again. This is thanks to special white blood cells called memory cells. They remember what your body needs to do to defeat the virus if it shows up again.

Hey, I know you!

1 When an unfamiliar virus enters your body, your immune system isn't properly prepared. The virus spreads and makes you feel sick.

3 Your white blood cells figure out how to defeat the virus. Your immune system is victorious! You start to feel better.

Fighting a virus

Your body fights viruses like it fights bad bacteria: with **white blood cells**. But did you know that your body can **learn from an infection**? Or that your doctor can give you a **head start** on fighting the next one?

2 Once the infection is detected by your immune system, white blood cells are sent in to do battle with the virus and learn its weaknesses.

4 Most of the white blood cells die now that their work is done, but some stick around. These are the memory cells. They hold on to a memory of the virus so they know how to defeat it if it comes back in the future.

This white blood cell will now remember the virus.

Vaccines

Doctors can inject you with a vaccine, which contains a weak version of a virus. Your white blood cells easily defeat the weakened virus, making new memory cells in the process. These cells will protect you if the real virus shows up.

Weakened virus cells

Deadly tricks

Viruses multiply by **taking over the cells** of an organism. However, to survive for a long time, they must **jump from one organism** to the next. Some viruses have developed tricks to help them make the leap.

Rabies

The rabies virus spreads when an infected animal, such as a dog, bites another creature. Amazingly, the infection makes the dog angrier and more likely to bite. This sneaky trick is what helps the virus spread.

Initial infection
A dog with rabies bites another dog. The virus passes from the saliva of the first dog into the bloodstream of the second.

1

4 Dangerous saliva
The virus travels down to the mouth, where saliva is made. The saliva the dog produces now contains the rabies virus. The cycle starts again when the dog bites another dog.

CAN VIRUSES GET WEAKER?

When a virus jumps from an animal to a human, it can cause serious illness. But viruses become less deadly over time. A virus weakens as our immune systems get used to it and become better at attacking it.

Lots of little rabies viruses attack the animal's cells.

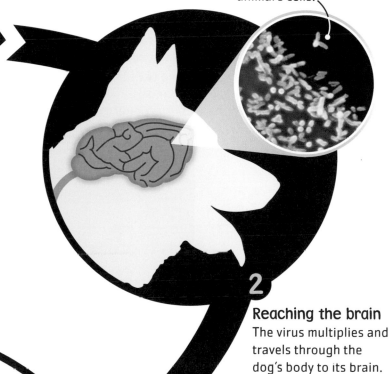

2 Reaching the brain
The virus multiplies and travels through the dog's body to its brain. Once in the brain, the virus causes swelling.

3 Bad behavior
Changes to the dog's brain cause its behavior to change. The dog becomes more aggressive and more likely to bite.

Zoonotic diseases

Though it is rare in humans, rabies is a zoonotic disease. This means it is a disease that can jump from an animal to a human. Zoonotic diseases are among the worst diseases in the world. Here are a few examples.

Avian flu
Avian flu, or bird flu, is a type of flu that usually spreads between birds. When the virus spreads to a human, it can be deadly.

West Nile fever
This virus is common in birds, such as crows. It can spread to humans via mosquito bites. Many infected people don't have any symptoms, but for some the virus causes illness.

Ebola
This life-threatening disease causes a high fever and bleeding in humans. Scientists believe the virus comes from bats.

Cat-scratch disease
Bacteria can cause zoonotic diseases, too. Cat scratch disease occurs when bacteria break into a human's body by a cat's scratch. This disease causes swelling and achy muscles.

Plant viruses

It's not just animals that get sick from viruses. **All living things** can suffer a virus attack, including plants. Because plants don't move from one place to another, plant viruses need to **find other ways to spread** from one victim to the next.

Sneaky scents

The cucumber mosaic virus has a clever way of spreading from plant to plant. It tricks the infected plant into making a powerful odor. The smell attracts plant-eating insects called aphids, who are drawn to the sweet scent every time.

1 What's that smell?
An aphid catches the strong scent of a nearby plant. It smells lush and full of delicious nutrients.

2 Flying toward food
Aphids swarm to the plant, ready for a yummy meal. When they get there, they take big bites.

3 Gross!
The plant is infected with a virus. When the aphids eat it, they also eat some of the virus—and it doesn't taste too good!

TULIP TROUBLE

Tulip petals are normally one color, but the tulip breaking virus causes them to grow with white stripes that "break" up the color. It may look cool, but this virus is harmful to the flower.

4 **Spreading the virus**
Disappointed by the taste, the aphids search for a better meal, taking the virus with them. When they find another plant and take a bite, the virus will spread.

CUCUMBER MOSAIC VIRUS

» The capsid, or shell, of the cucumber mosaic virus is shaped kind of like a soccer ball. It is made of 12 five-sided pentagons and 20 six-sided hexagons.

What are fungi?

There are lots of different types of **fungus**, but they all have something in common: They get their nutrients from other organisms, **dead and alive**, by oozing fluid onto them and then sucking the nutrients back up.

Mold

A lot of microbes are made of one cell, but mold, a type of fungus, is different. A few cells stick together to form threads that look like branches. They use these threads to feed on nutrients, like those in this piece of fungus-covered bread.

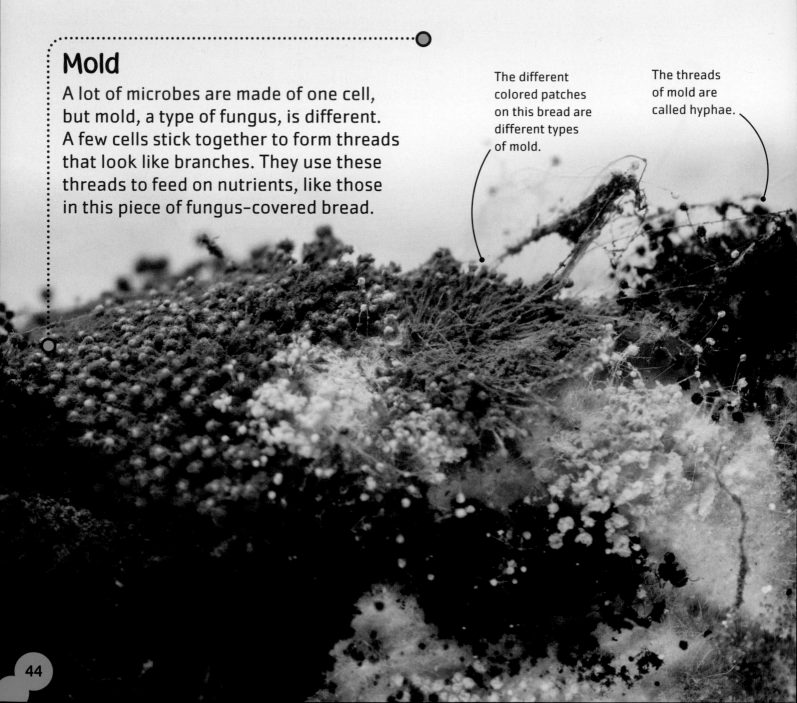

The different colored patches on this bread are different types of mold.

The threads of mold are called hyphae.

BLACK BREAD MOLD (RHIZOPUS STOLONIFER)

Funky fungi

You can find different types of fungus, such as molds, yeasts, and mushrooms, growing anywhere it is warm and damp, including on our bodies!

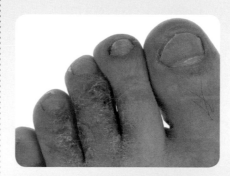

Fungal infection
Some fungi grow on our bodies and cause diseases like athlete's foot. They thrive in the moist conditions inside sweaty shoes.

Dried yeast
Yeast is a fungus used as an ingredient in baking. It makes bubbles of carbon dioxide gas that help make air pockets in foods such as bread.

Mushrooms
Some fungi feed unseen underground until they are ready to reproduce. Then they pop out onto the surface as mushrooms.

FEELING CRABBY

To be considered a fungus, a microbe's cell walls must be made of a material called chitin. Chitin is the same substance that crab shells and insect exoskeletons are made of.

Mega mold

Floating in the air around us are tiny, dust-sized specks called **spores**. When they land on food, they start to grow and multiply into **big patches** of a fungus: **mold**.

Yuck! Mold has taken over completely, and the tomato needs to be thrown away.

Getting moldy

After a tomato is picked from its plant, the clock starts ticking. How long do you have before the mold takes over?

Freshly picked
The cells of the tomato are strong. Mold spores are unable to get through the tough skin.

After one week
Without a fresh supply of nutrients from its plant, the tomato becomes weak and starts to break down.

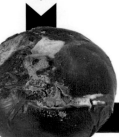

After two weeks
Mold appears as it feeds on the nutrients released by the rotting tomato.

Slow it down

We store food in fridges to help keep it fresh. The cold temperatures slow down both the growth of the mold and the natural ripening and decay of the fruit, so mold can't get in.

After four weeks

The tomato becomes soft and mushy as the mold eats it.

Mold isn't always bad for you. We even grow mold on purpose sometimes. So what should you look out for?

Mold in your home

Mold often grows around taps and other damp spots in your home. Too much can cause allergic reactions. Bad!

Spoiled food

Unwanted mold is a sign that food has spoiled, so there may be other dangerous microbes in there. Avoid!

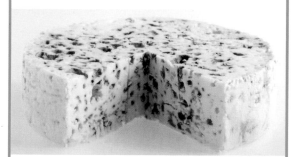

Tasty mold

A special, edible mold is grown in some foods, such as blue cheese, to give it a strong, tangy flavor. Yum!

Growing and spreading

Mold seems to **appear from nowhere**. One day the apples in your fruit bowl are **shiny and red**, and the next day, a patch of green fur appears on them. **Where does this fungus come from?**

Spores grow
As food rots, nutrients are released. Mold spores use these nutrients to grow.

2

Cycle of spores
Fungi like mold use cells called spores to spread. A new organism can grow from each one. Spores are very light and tough, so they can survive long journeys floating in the air.

1

Spores land
The air is full of mold spores, so you'll find them settling on most surfaces, including on food.

DANDELION SEEDS

Spores are a lot like seeds. Just like dandelion seeds, for example, mold spores are spread by the wind. Where they land, a new organism grows.

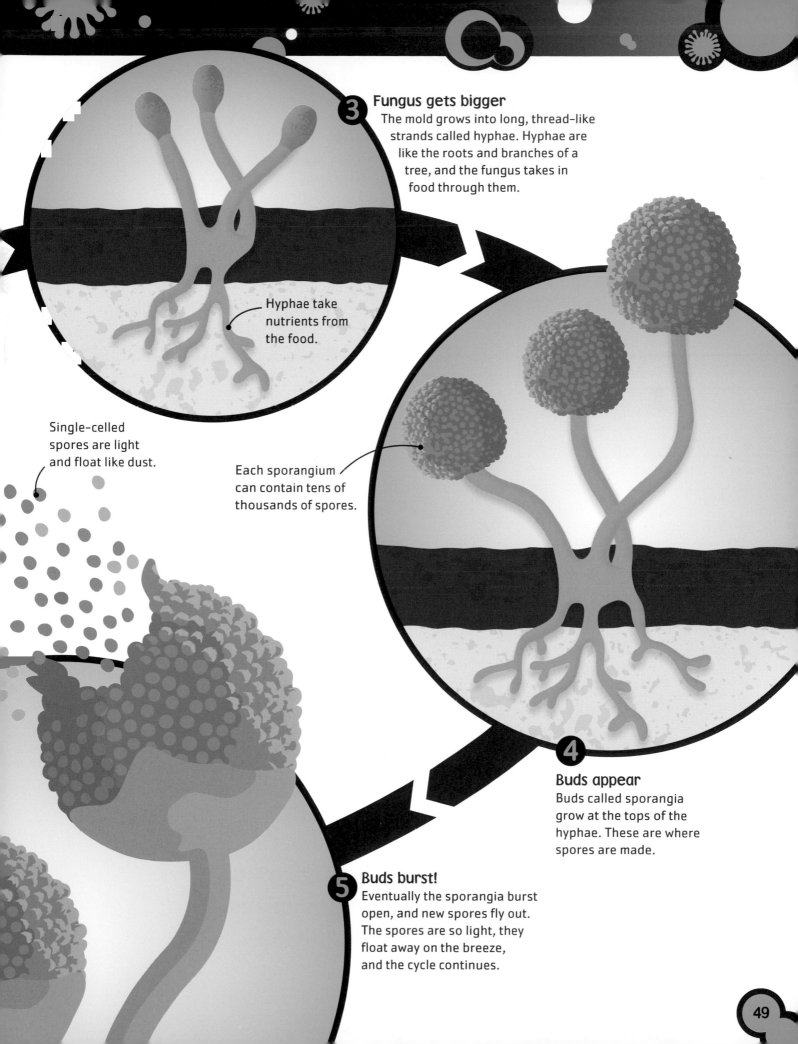

③ Fungus gets bigger
The mold grows into long, thread-like strands called hyphae. Hyphae are like the roots and branches of a tree, and the fungus takes in food through them.

Hyphae take nutrients from the food.

Single-celled spores are light and float like dust.

Each sporangium can contain tens of thousands of spores.

④ Buds appear
Buds called sporangia grow at the tops of the hyphae. These are where spores are made.

⑤ Buds burst!
Eventually the sporangia burst open, and new spores fly out. The spores are so light, they float away on the breeze, and the cycle continues.

Fermentation

Yeasts are a type of fungus made of one cell. They change sugars into other molecules, such as alcohol and carbon dioxide gas, through fermentation. This is why people use yeast to make drinks like wine.

1 The first step in making wine involves crushing a lot of grapes. Traditionally people did this by stamping on the grapes with their feet!

2 Grapes have natural yeast on their skins. Crushing them mixes the yeast with the sugar inside. This starts the process of fermentation.

3 The yeast dies when the amount of alcohol becomes too high for it. If the wine is bottled before the yeast dies, bubbles of carbon dioxide are trapped, making it fizzy.

Micro chefs

Who would have thought microbes could also be **helpful** in the kitchen? We've been using fungi and bacteria in a process called **fermentation** for **thousands of years**. This process makes food last longer and makes it more delicious.

Favorite foods

Fermentation is used in a few unexpected products. Here are some of the world's favorite fermented foods.

The holes in bread are made by carbon dioxide gas.

Kimchi

Kimchi is a traditional Korean side dish made from cabbage and other vegetables. Bacteria ferment the cabbage to give it a sour taste.

Bread

Yeast is added to bread dough to make bubbles of carbon dioxide. The gas is trapped in the dough, and that's what makes bread light and fluffy.

Cheese

When one of the sugars in milk, called lactose, is fermented using bacteria, it makes lactic acid. Lactic acid is what gives cheese its tangy flavor.

Yogurt

Like cheese, yogurt is made by fermenting the sugars in milk. One of the main microbes responsible is a bacteria called Lactobacillus (lak-toh-bah-SILL-us).

Mind control

When the spores of a certain fungus, called Ophiocordyceps unilateralis, land on an ant, they spread through the ant's body. Before long, the fungus will completely take over the ant's mind and behavior.

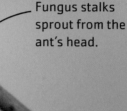

The balls of fungus at the end of the stalks, called sporangia, will burst, releasing lots and lots of spores.

Fungus stalks sprout from the ant's head.

❶ Spores land
Spores fall from a fungus and land on an ant. They use special chemicals called enzymes to break into the ant's body.

❸ Ant climbs
The fungus forces the ant to climb up to the top of a plant and bite down hard.

❷ Fungus infects
The fungus cells multiply and spread through the ant. They release more chemicals that change the ant's behavior.

Zombie ants!

We normally think of fungi growing on dead plants and animals. However, some can grow inside **living creatures**, and even **change their behavior**. One freaky fungus even turns ants into zombies.

④ Fungus sprouts

Now anchored to the plant by its strong jaws, the ant dies. The fungus growing inside the ant bursts out in long stalks.

⑤ Cycle continues

The fungus releases more spores, which fall onto other unsuspecting ants below, making new zombie ants.

The ant stays anchored to the plant even after it dies.

FUNGUS FARMERS

Not all fungi are bad for ants. In fact, leaf-cutting ants grow fungi like crops. They take pieces of leaves to their undergroud nests. When fungus grows on the leaves, the ants farm it and eat it.

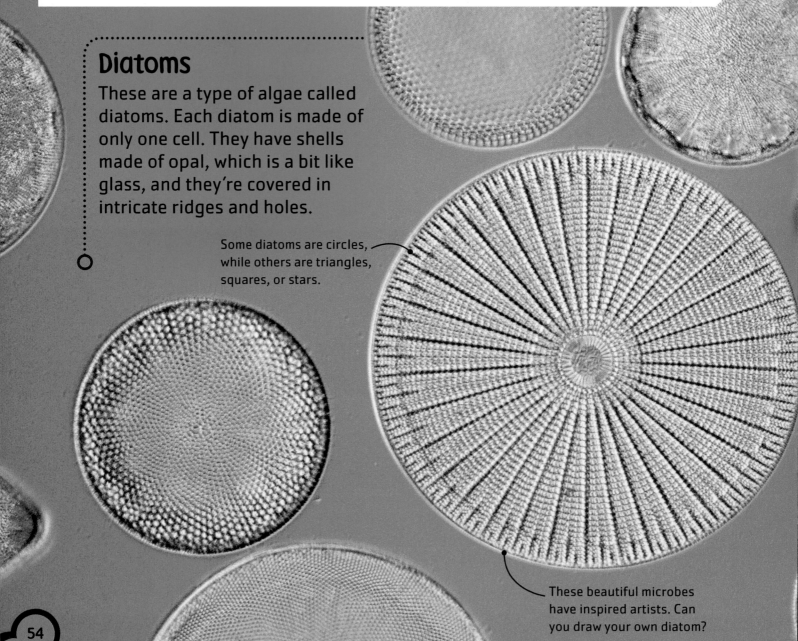

What are
algae?

Have you ever seen what looks like green slime growing on a **lake or pond**? That's probably algae! This microbe is known for its color—but not all algae are green. The variety of these **amazing creatures** may surprise you.

Diatoms

These are a type of algae called diatoms. Each diatom is made of only one cell. They have shells made of opal, which is a bit like glass, and they're covered in intricate ridges and holes.

Some diatoms are circles, while others are triangles, squares, or stars.

These beautiful microbes have inspired artists. Can you draw your own diatom?

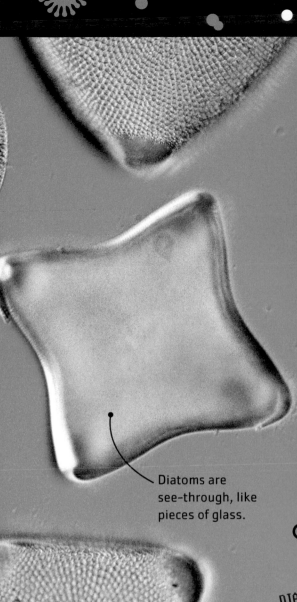

Zoochlorella and kelp

Algae come in many different shapes and sizes, from single-celled microscopic creatures to giant multi-celled seaweed.

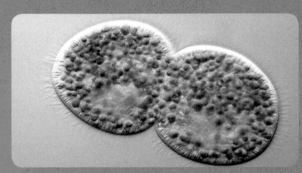

Zoochlorella
Each of these teeny green blobs is its own single-celled algae called zoochlorella. Zoochlorella only live inside other creatures.

Kelp
Kelp is a type of algae called seaweed. It is usually brown and grows underwater in giant forests.

Diatoms are see-through, like pieces of glass.

DIATOM SHELL SPECKLED WITH HOLES

In and out

The hard shell of a diatom is impermeable—nothing can flow through it. That's why it's covered in small holes. The holes let in nutrients and let out waste products.

Growing green

All algae have the same energy source. Just like plants, algae get energy from **the sun** in a process called **photosynthesis**. During this process, they also take in carbon dioxide gas and use it to make **oxygen**.

Algal bloom

When the temperature, sunlight, and other conditions are just right, algae can take over a pond, a lake, or even a large area of the ocean. These big, green bodies are called algal blooms, and they're quite a sight.

GREEN FRESHWATER ALGAE

Look closer
These freshwater algae are green because of special molecules inside them called chlorophyll. The chlorophyll helps with photosynthesis.

About half of the **oxygen** we breathe is **made by algae!**

Algae are like the trees and grass of our oceans, lakes, ponds, and rivers. Like plants, they take in sunlight and use it to make sugar and oxygen.

Energy from the sun

The chlorophyll molecules inside algae take in energy from the sun and store it as sugar. Algae can use the sugar to move and grow. Some animals, such as this snail, eat algae. They want to use the high-energy sugar to move and grow, too!

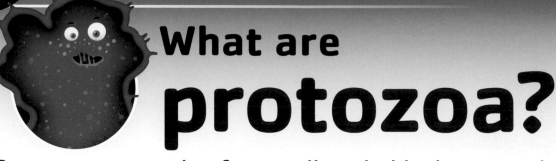

What are protozoa?

Protozoa are made of one cell each, like bacteria, but they are actually more **closely related to plants and animals**. They behave like animals, too, by moving around and **eating other living things**.

Amoeba

An amoeba is a type of protozoa that looks like a splotch of jelly and can change shape constantly. It moves and eats by sending out leg-like limbs. Some amoebas prey on and eat other simple organisms, such as bacteria.

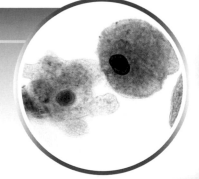

AMOEBAS

>> Amoebas can sense chemicals given off by their food. This is like our sense of smell.

The **cell membrane** of an amoeba is very flexible and fluid.

Cytoplasm makes up most of the inside of an amoeba.

The amoeba's **DNA** is found in a central pouch called a **nucleus**.

1 The amoeba sends out limbs to completely surround a bacteria.

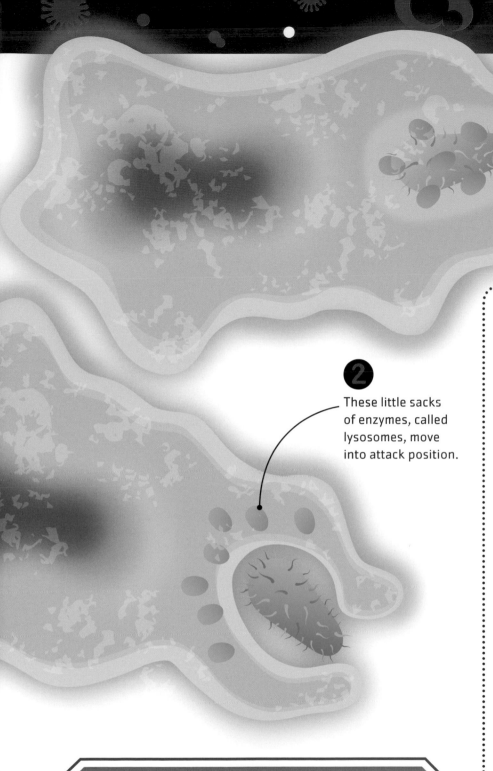

3 Once the bacteria is fully captured, the lysosomes release their enzymes. They break down the bacteria into nutrients, which are taken in by the amoeba as food.

2 These little sacks of enzymes, called lysosomes, move into attack position.

Protozoa pals

As well as amoebas, there are two other major types of protozoa. They are the ciliates and the flagellates.

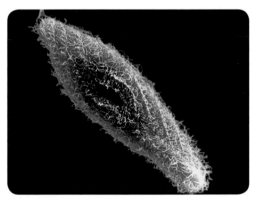

Ciliates
Ciliates are covered in hair-like strands called cilia. They use them to move, eat, sense, and hold on to things.

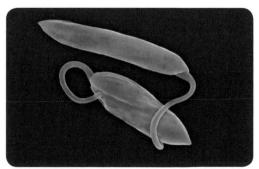

Flagellates
Flagellates have at least one long tail, called a flagellum, that they use to swim. Some flagellates cause diseases in humans.

THAT'S HUGE!

Most creatures made of one cell are tiny, but not all. This amoeba is called a xenophyophore (zen-oh-FI-oh-fore). It's the biggest single-celled organism we know. It can grow up to 8 in (20 cm) across—bigger than your hand!

What are archaea?

Archaea also look a lot like bacteria, but their **cell membranes** are super strong. Archaea are known for being able to live in **really extreme places** where other microbes couldn't survive.

Hot stuff

Some archaea live in temperatures around 212°F (100°C)! They are called hyperthermophiles. High temperatures cause important molecules like DNA to break, so hyperthermophiles need to be really good at fixing broken molecules.

The **cell membrane** of a hyperthermophile is strong to help it survive extreme heat, such as near an underwater vent.

What is an underwater vent?
Water seeps into cracks in the ocean floor where it's heated by hot rocks and magma. It then emerges in places called hydrothermal vents, which are like underwater volcanoes. Hyperthermophiles can be found living here.

Archaea can have more than one **flagellum**, or tail, to help them move around.

Extreme archaea

Archaea aren't only found living in high temperatures. Some archaea have made their home in other extreme environments.

Where hot water from the vent meets cold water in the ocean, dark "smoke" forms.

Hot water spews out the top of an underwater vent.

Surviving salt
Scientists used to think nothing could survive in really salty water. However, some archaea can live in water that is 10 times saltier than the ocean.

Resisting radiation
Certain types of archaea can survive 3,000 times the exposure to a kind of energy, called radiation, that would kill a human. These creatures are truly tough.

There are **no diseases** caused by archaea.

MICROBE RAINBOW

Not all extreme microbes are archaea. These beautiful rainbow colors circling the Grand Prismatic Spring at Yellowstone National Park in Wyoming are actually created by heat-loving bacteria.

Micro animals

Not all microorganisms are made of a single cell, like bacteria and protozoa. Some are **made of many cells** but are still too small to see. We call the creepy-crawly ones **micro animals**! Meet a few of them here.

These are mite tails poking out from inside an eyelash follicle.

Eyelash mites

Half of all people have demodex living in their eyelashes. Demodex are a type of animal called a mite that are about 0.02 in (0.4 mm) long. They have eight legs and walk around on our eyelids at night.

Nematode worm

Ninety percent of the animals on the ocean floor are tiny creatures called nematode worms. They can also live inside people and other animals. Nematodes eat plants and other microbes, such as bacteria.

The **smallest** nematodes are still **40 times longer** than E. coli bacteria.

Most nematodes are under 0.1 in (2.5 mm) long.

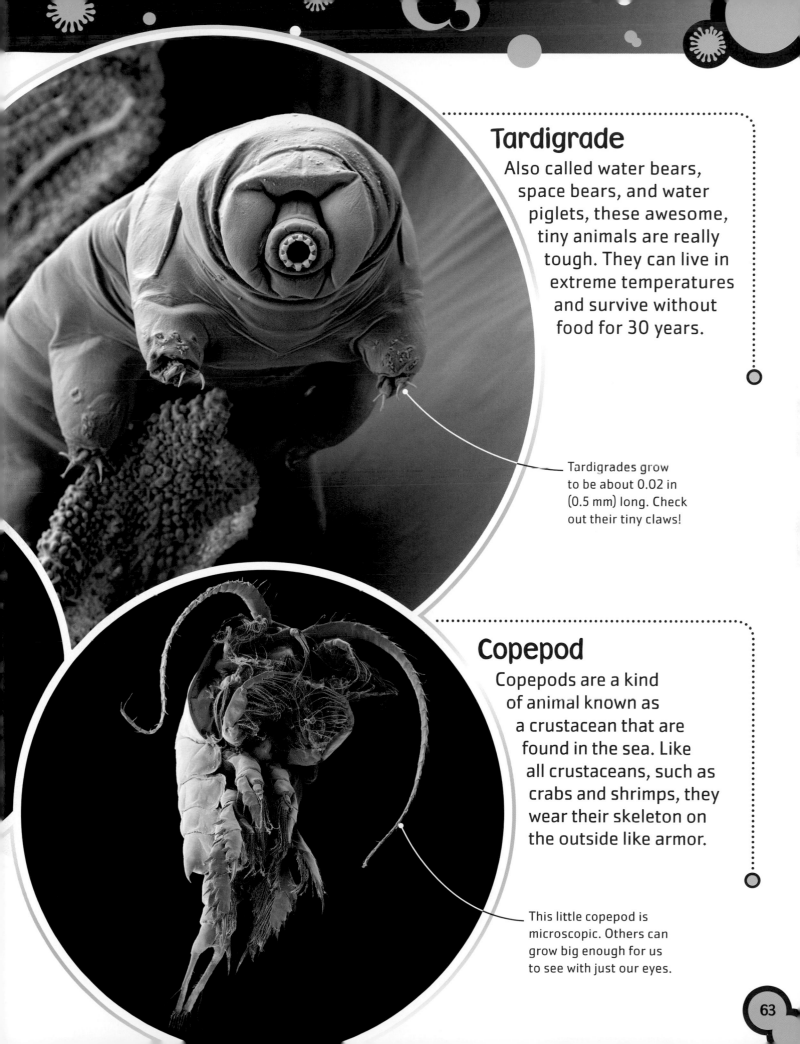

Tardigrade

Also called water bears, space bears, and water piglets, these awesome, tiny animals are really tough. They can live in extreme temperatures and survive without food for 30 years.

Tardigrades grow to be about 0.02 in (0.5 mm) long. Check out their tiny claws!

Copepod

Copepods are a kind of animal known as a crustacean that are found in the sea. Like all crustaceans, such as crabs and shrimps, they wear their skeleton on the outside like armor.

This little copepod is microscopic. Others can grow big enough for us to see with just our eyes.

Timeline of microbiology

What we know about **microbes** and microbiology has changed over the years. Here are just a few of the most **important moments and discoveries**.

KIRCHER

Model of Hooke's microscope

SPIROGYRA ALGAE

1656

1665

1670s

Microbes

Looking for a cure for the **plague** in Rome, Italy, scholar Athanasius **Kircher** is the first person to **observe microbes** under a microscope. He figures out that they are the cause of **diseases**.

Mold spores

Scientist Robert **Hooke** is the first person to observe and write about **mold spores**. He also comes up with the word "**cell**" when he notices that cork cells under a microscope look like the **rooms**, or **cells**, in a monastery.

Bacteria

Scientist Anton van **Leeuwenhoek** is the first person to describe **bacteria** in 1676. He later discovers **Spirogyra**, a type of algae, as well as tiny **nematode** worms. Today, Leeuwenhoek is known as the "**Father of Microbiology**."

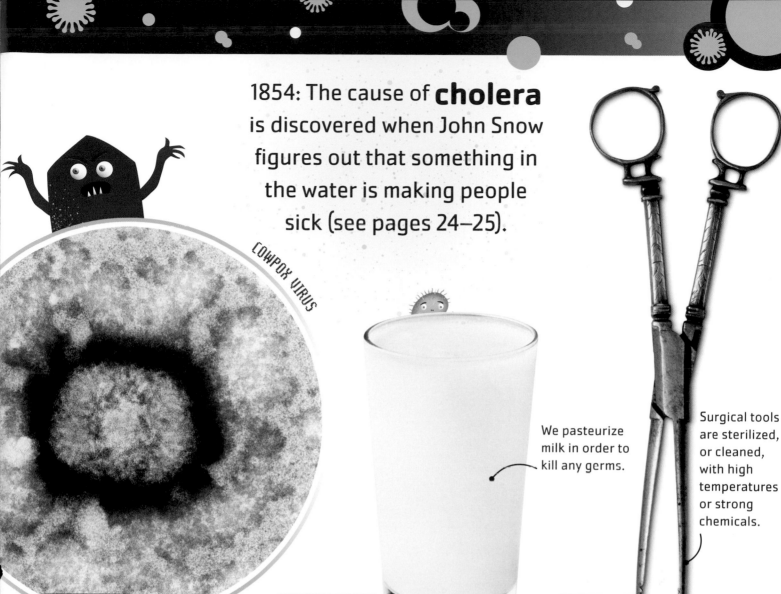

1854: The cause of **cholera** is discovered when John Snow figures out that something in the water is making people sick (see pages 24–25).

COWPOX VIRUS

We pasteurize milk in order to kill any germs.

Surgical tools are sterilized, or cleaned, with high temperatures or strong chemicals.

1796

Vaccines

Physician Edward **Jenner** shows that the **cowpox virus** is harmless to humans and it gives them immunity to **smallpox**, a terrible disease. This is the first-ever vaccine. In fact, the word "**vaccine**" comes from the Latin word for **cow**!

1862

Germs

Biologist Louis **Pasteur** proves that germs don't show up **randomly**. They **spread** from one place to another. He shows this by heating broths to kill the **germs**. He perfects this process, and we now know it as **pasteurization**.

1865

Sterilization

Inspired by Pasteur, surgeon Joseph **Lister** comes up with the idea of **sterilization** to prevent infection during surgery. This includes **washing hands**, disinfecting wounds, and cleaning surgical instruments such as **scalpels**.

1928: Alexander Fleming discovers **penicillin** (see pages 28–29).

These germ cells are being eaten up by a macrophage.

TOBACCO MOSAIC VIRUS

STAINED BACTERIA

DISEASED LEAVES

1880s

Staining

Physician Robert **Koch** invents a way to stain bacteria different **colors**. This makes them easier to see under a **microscope** and helps him identify the bacteria that causes the disease **tuberculosis**.

1883

Macrophages

Zoologist (animal scientist) Ilya **Mechnikov** observes cells eating other cells. This act is called **phagocytosis**, and it's how some of the white blood cells in our body, called **macrophages**, fight infection—by **eating** the **intruding** germs!

1892

Viruses

Botanist (plant scientist) Dmitri **Ivanovsky** and microbiologist Martinus **Beijerinck** discover a disease in plants that is spread by something **smaller** than bacteria: the **tobacco mosaic virus**. This is the first virus ever discovered.

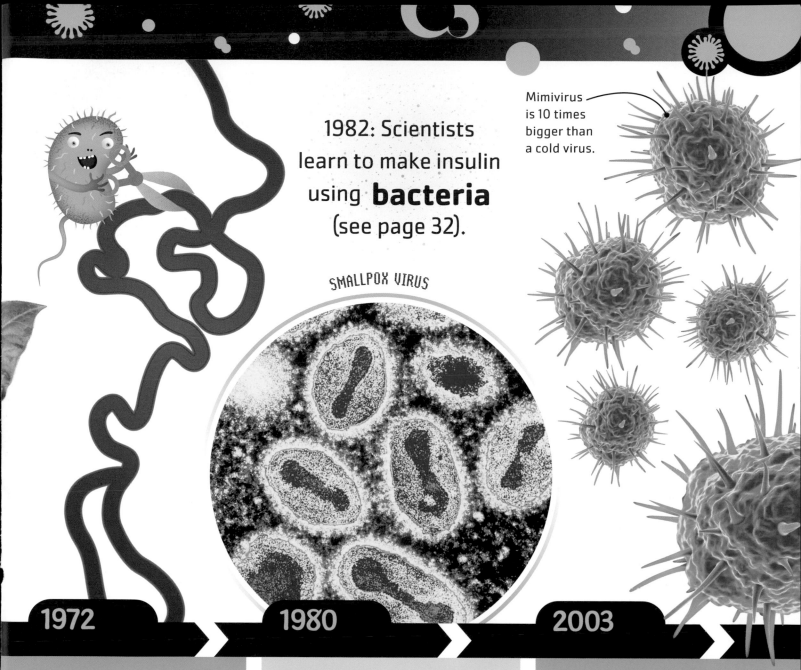

Mimivirus is 10 times bigger than a cold virus.

1982: Scientists learn to make insulin using **bacteria** (see page 32).

SMALLPOX VIRUS

1972

Genes

Biochemists Stanley **Cohen** and Herbert **Boyer** use enzymes to copy bits of **DNA** from one organism to another. This is the start of **genetic engineering**, or changing the DNA of an organism to affect how it **behaves**.

1980

Smallpox

For the first time ever, a **disease** is completely destroyed worldwide. **Smallpox** is no longer a threat thanks to a global **vaccine** effort. Samples of the **virus** are still kept in laboratories so **scientists** can use them for **research**, but some people think even they should be destroyed.

2003

More to learn!

Biologist Didier **Raoult** finds a very large virus, **Mimivirus**, that acts differently than other viruses. This discovery makes scientists question what a **virus** really is—which just goes to show, there's a **lot more still to learn** about microbiology!

Glossary

These words are helpful to know when talking and learning about bacteria and microbiology.

adenovirus (AD-e-noh-VI-ruhs)
type of virus that affects an organism's breathing

agar (AH-gur)
jelly-like substance used to grow microbes in petri dishes

algae (AL-jee)
microbes that use chlorophyll to take in energy from the sun

amoeba (ah-MEE-buh)
type of protozoa that easily changes its shape

antibiotics
medicines that fight bacteria

archaea (ahr-KAY-uh)
microbes that are a lot like bacteria, but with different characteristics and strong cell membranes

bacilli (buh-SIL-i)
rod-shaped bacteria

bacteria
most common group of microbes

bacteriologist (bak-teer-ee-OL-uh-jist)
scientist who studies bacteria

bacteriophage (bak-TEER-ee-uh-fayj)
type of virus that attacks bacteria

bioluminescence (bi-oh-loo-muh-NES-uhns)
organism's ability to give off light

cell
basic building block of organisms

cell membrane
layer that holds a cell together and allows substances in and out

cell wall
extra layer of protection around some cell membranes

chitin (KI-tin)
material that makes up the cell walls of all fungi

chlorophyll (KLAWR-uh-fill)
chemical used in photosynthesis

cholera (KOL-er-uh)
terrible illness that can spread in unclean conditions

ciliates (SIL-ee-ates)
type of protozoa covered in hair-like strands

cocci (KOK-si)
round-shaped bacteria

contaminated
substance that has had something harmful like germs added to it

crustacean (kruhs-TAY-shun)
group of animals that includes copepods, crabs, and shrimps

cytoplasm (SY-to-plaz-uhm)
jelly-like substance inside cells

diatom (DI-ah-tom)
type of algae made of one cell

digestive system
system through which an organism, such as a human, breaks down and uses its food

DNA
molecule inside a cell that tells the organism how to act

ebola (ee-BO-luh)
type of virus that is very deadly

enzymes (EN-zimes)
chemicals that break down large molecules into smaller molecules

fermentation
process by which microbes change sugars into other substances

flagellates (FLAJ-uh-lets)
type of protozoa with a long flagellum

flagellum (fluh-JEL-uhm)
tail some microbes have to help them to move

fungi (FUN-ji or FUN-guy)
microbes that reproduce by making and spreading spores

germs
harmful microbes that can make people sick

hyperthermophile (hi-per-THUR-mo-file)
type of archaea that can survive in very high temperatures like those near underwater vents

hyphae (HI-fee)
thread-like strands of fungus

immune system
system through which an organism gets rid of invaders, such as germs

influenza (in-floo-WEN-zuh)
type of virus that causes the flu

insulin
chemical that balances the level of sugar in an organism's blood

macrophage (MAK-roh-fayj)
white blood cell that eats germs

memory cell
white blood cell that remembers an infection after it has gone

micro animal
animals that are too small to see without a microscope

microbe
shorter word for "microorganism"

microbiology
science of microorganisms

microorganism
any living creature that is too small to see without a microscope

microscope
tool that uses curved glass to make things look bigger

molecule
smallest amount of any substance

mold
type of fuzzy fungus that grows in moist places such as on rotting food

Mould, Steve
author of this book!

nitrogen
type of gas in the atmosphere

nutrients
substances found in food that an organism uses to grow

oligosaccharides (ol-eh-goh-SAK-uh-rides)
long molecules found in some foods, such as beans

Ophiocordyceps unilateralis (oh-FI-o-KOR-deh-seps yoo-nuh-LAH-tur-uhl-us)
zombie-ant fungus

organism
any living creature

pasteurization (pas-chur-i-ZAY-shun)
process of heating liquids, such as milk, to kill any germs living inside

penicillin (pen-uh-SIL-in)
antibiotic substance produced by a type of mold

petri dish
special plate on which scientists grow microbes

phagocytosis (fahg-o-si-TOH-sis)
act of one cell eating another, such as how macrophages eat germs

photosynthesis
process by which plants and algae take in energy from the sun

pili
little hairs on the outside of some bacteria used to attach to surfaces

protozoa (pro-tuh-ZO-uh)
group of single-celled microbes that eat other organisms

reproduction
how one organism makes more organisms

ribosomes
molecules in a cell that build parts for the organism

spirilla (spi-RIL-uh)
spiral-shaped bacteria

Spirogyra (SPY-ro-JI-ruh)
type of slimy algae

sporangia (spo-RAN-jee-ah)
balls of spores on a fungus

spore
seed-like cell that spreads a fungus

sterilization (ster-uh-lie-ZAY-shuhn)
process of cleaning objects like surgical tools to kill germs

symptoms
signs of a disease, such as sneezing or swelling

toxins
dangerous chemicals

vaccine
substance that contains a weak version of a virus. Doctors inject people with vaccines to protect against harmful diseases

virus
microbe that infects the cells of organisms and causes disease

yeast
type of fungus made of just one cell. Yeast is used in fermentation

zoochlorella (zoo-oh-kluh-REL-uh)
type of algae that only lives inside other creatures

zoonotic (zoo-uh-NOT-ik)
diseases that pass from animals to humans

Index

Aa

acne 25
adenovirus 35
agar 11
air 18
algae 9, 54–57
allergies 27, 47
amoebas 9, 58–59
anglerfish 21
animal-borne viruses 40–41
animals 12, 19, 62–63
antibiotics 28–29
ants 52–53
aphids 42–43
archaea 9, 60–61
atmosphere 18
Avian flu 41

Bb

bacilli 15
bacteria 6, 7, 8, 11, 13,
    14–25, 30–33, 64
bacteriophages 7, 8, 34
bioluminescence 20–21
blood 26–27
bobtail squid 20–21
bread 51

Cc

carbon dioxide 50, 51, 56
cat scratch disease 41
cell membranes 13, 15, 34,
    58, 60
cells 12–13, 14–15, 38–39
cell wall 14, 34, 45
cheese 47, 51
chitin 45

chlorophyll 9, 56–57
cholera 24–25, 65
ciliates 59
cleaning products 33
clouds 18
cocci 15
colds 36–37
copepods 63
crops 33, 53
cucumber mosaic virus
    42–43
cuts 26
cytoplasm 13, 15, 58

Dd

diabetes 32
diarrhea 24, 25
diatoms 54–55
digestion 22–23
diseases 24–25, 34–35,
    36–41, 64–65
dissolving 31
DNA 13, 15, 16, 32, 33, 34, 35,
    58, 60

Ee

ebola 35, 41
E. coli 16–17
electrical charge 30
electron microscopes 11
enzymes 23, 33, 52, 59
eyelash mites 62

Ff

farts 22, 23
fermentation 50–51
fertilizers 19

fevers 27
flagellates 59
flagellum 15, 60
Fleming, Alexander 28–29,
    66
follicles 25
food 46–51
fox fire 21
fridges 47
fungi 9, 21, 44–53

Gg

genes 67
germs 11, 19, 24–25, 26, 65
Grand Prismatic Spring 61

Hh

hand-washing 37
homes 19
human body 12, 19, 22–23
hydrothermal vents 60–61
hyperthermophiles 9, 60
hyphae 44, 49

Ii

immune system 26–27,
    38–39, 41
infection 26–27, 38–41
influenza 35
insect-borne viruses 42–43
insulin 32, 67
intestines 23

Kk

kelp 55
kimchi 51

Acknowledgments

DK would like to thank the following: Sakshi Saluja for picture research; Yamini Panwar, Pankaj Sharma, and Rizwan Mohd for hi-res assistance; Kasey Greenbaum and Katy Lennon for editorial assistance; Polly Goodman for proofreading; and Helen Peters for the index.

Steve Mould would like to dedicate this book to his growing family: Lianne, Ella, Lyra, and Aster.

The publisher would like to thank the following for their kind permission to reproduce their photographs:

(Key: a-above; b-below/bottom; c-center; f-far; l-left; r-right; t-top)

4–5 Science Photo Library: Science Photo Library. **6 123RF.com:** Maya Kovacheva (bl). **8 Science Photo Library:** Biozentrum, University Of Basel (br); Dennis Kunkel Microscopy (cl). **9 Science Photo Library:** Wim Van Egmond (tl); Dennis Kunkel Microscopy (cl); Jannicke Wiik-Nielsen (cr); Derek Lovley / Kazem Kashefi (bl). **10 Getty Images:** De Agostini (crb); Klaus Vedfelt (cl). **11 Alamy Stock Photo:** Phanie (tr). **Getty Images:** Monty Rakusen (tl). **13 Science Photo Library:** Daniela Beckmann (cra). **15 Science Photo Library:** Steve Gschmeissner (cra/Bacilli); Science Photo Library (cra); Dennis Kunkel Microscopy (cr). **17 Science Photo Library:** Steve Gschmeissner (tr). **18 123RF.com:** rangizzz (bc). **Dreamstime. com:** Ulkass (cb). **Getty Images:** Westend61 (cr). **19 Dreamstime.com:** Okea (cl). **Getty Images:** KidStock (bc). **iStockphoto.com:** NicolasMcComber (cb). **20–21 Alamy Stock Photo:** Stocktrek Images, Inc. **21 Alamy Stock Photo:** Doug Perrine (crb). **Getty Images:** Lance@ ancelpics (cra). **naturepl.com:** David Shale (cr). **24 Science Photo Library:** Ktsdesign (clb). **27 123RF.com:** Parinya Binsuk (cr). **Alamy Stock Photo:** Mediscan (tc); Christopher Stewart (crb). **Dreamstime. com:** Photoeuphoria (cra). **Science Photo Library:** Science Photo Library (cla). **28 Getty Images:** Chris Ware / Stringer (cra, bl). **29 Getty Images:** Bettmann (cla); Uladzimir Sarokin / EyeEm (cra). **30 Science Photo Library:** Dennis Kunkel Microscopy (cl, bc). **31 Alamy Stock Photo:** Science History Images (tr). **Science Photo Library:** Dante Fenolio (br); Steve Gschmeissner (c). **33 Alamy Stock Photo:** Nigel Cattlin (tr); US Coast Guard Photo (crb). **Dreamstime.com:** Atorn Buaksantiah (cla); Roman Suslenko (clb). **35 Science Photo Library:** James Cavallini (tc); Dr Linda Stannard (tc/Adenovirus); A. Dowsett, Health Protection Agency (tr). **36 Science Photo Library:** A.B. Dowsett (cra). **39 Getty Images:** Blend Images (bc). **41 Science Photo Library:** Dr Gopal Murti (cl). **42–43 Alamy Stock Photo:** Nigel Cattlin (c). **43 123RF.com:** Irina Opachevsky (tr). **Getty Images:** Science Picture Co (crb). **44–45 Dreamstime.com:** Hadkhanong (b). **45 Dreamstime.com:** Carroteater (cra); Peter Wollinga (crb). **Science Photo Library:** Dr Jeremy Burgess (cla). **47 Alamy Stock Photo:** Patricia Phillips / Stockimo (cra). **Dreamstime.com:** Gcpics (cr). **48 Alamy Stock Photo:** Brian Jackson (cb). **52–53 Getty Images:** Piotr Naskrecki (c). **53 Dreamstime.com:** Pablo Hidalgo / Pxhidalgo (br). **54–55 Getty Images:** Darlyne A. Murawski (c). **55 Dreamstime.com:** Ethan Daniels (cra/Giant Kelp Forest). **Science Photo Library:** Wim Van Egmond (cra/ Paramecium bursaria); Steve Gschmeissner (cb). **56 Getty Images:** Frank Fox (bl). **56–57 Getty Images:** Sharon Vos-Arnold (c). **57 Alamy Stock Photo:** blickwinkel (br). **58 Alamy Stock Photo:** Papilio (cra). **59 Getty Images:** Dr. Karl Aufderheide (cr). **Science Photo Library:** Dennis Kunkel Microscopy (crb). **60 Science Photo Library:** Eye of Science (c). **61 Alamy Stock Photo:** Michael Ventura (ca). **Dreamstime.com:** Minyun Zhou / Minyun9260 (br). **Getty Images:** lappes (cra). **62 Science Photo Library:** Steve Gschmeissner (cra); Dr. Richard Kessel & Dr. Gene Shih (crb). **63 Science Photo Library:** Steve Gschmeissner (b); Eye of Science (tl). **64 Dorling Kindersley:** Dave King / The Science Museum (ca). **Science Photo Library:** Collection Abecasis (cla); Marek Mis (cra). **65 Dorling Kindersley:** David Exton / Science Museum, London / David Exton / Science Museum, London / Science Museum, London (cra). **Getty Images:** Heather Davies / SPL (cla). **66 Getty Images:** Nigel Cattlin (cra). **Science Photo Library:** Cnri (cl); Kateryna Kon (ca); Dennis Kunkel Microscopy (tr). **67 Science Photo Library:** Mehau Kulyk (cra); Eye of Science (c)

Cover images: Front: Getty Images: Steve Gschmeissner / Science cb; **Science Photo Library:** Dennis Kunkel Microscopy cla, A.B. Dowsett bc, Dr Linda Stannard bl; Back: **Science Photo Library:** James Cavallini tr, Ktsdesign cl, Science Photo Library cb; **Steve Ullathorne:** clb

All other images © Dorling Kindersley
For further information see:
www.dkimages.com